D1604839

From Graphite to Pencil

From Graphite to Pencil

Ali Mitgutsch

 Carolrhoda Books, Inc., Minneapolis

674
Mit

First published in the United States of America 1985 by Carolrhoda Books, Inc.
Original edition © 1982 by Sellier Verlag GmbH, Eching bei München,
West Germany, under the title VOM GRAPHIT ZUM BLEISTIFT
Revised English text © 1985 by Carolrhoda Books, Inc.
Illustrations © 1982 by Sellier Verlag GmbH

Manufactured in the United States of America

LIBRARY OF CONGRESS CATALOGING IN PUBLICATION DATA

Mitgutsch, Ali.
    From graphite to pencil.

        (A Carolrhoda start to finish book)
        Rev. English text of: Vom Graphit zum Bleistift.
        SUMMARY: Describes the process by which graphite
becomes a pencil from the making of the graphite to the
way it is encased in cedar and topped with an eraser.

        1. Pencils — Juvenile literature. [1. Pencils]
I. Title.   II. Series.

TS1268.M5813   1985   674'.88   84-17469
ISBN 0-87614-231-5 (lib. bdg.)

    1 2   3   4   5   6   7   8   9   10 94 93 92 91 90 89 88 87 86 85

From Graphite to Pencil

Over 2½ billion pencils
are sold in the United States every year.
That's about 11 pencils for each person in the country.
Where do all these pencils come from?
The wooden cases for most pencils
are made from the trunks of cedar trees.
Cedar makes pencils that are easy to sharpen
without splitting them.

The most important part of a pencil is what's inside.

People often call pencils **lead pencils**,

but there's really no lead in them.

The lead is made from a mixture of **graphite** and **clay**.

Like real lead, graphite is dark gray.

It is found in mines deep beneath the ground.

The graphite is mixed with clay and water
in a high-speed mixer.
The more clay that is used, the harder the lead will be.
The less clay used, the softer and blacker the lead will be.

Next the mixture is molded into a long string of lead.
The lead is then cut into pieces about 7¼ inches long.
These short pieces of lead are still soft
like thin licorice sticks.

These pieces of lead are now baked in a very hot oven.
After they have cooled, the leads will be hard,
but they will also be rough like sandpaper.
To make them smooth, they are dipped in wax.
This makes them glide easily over paper.

Now it is time to put the leads into their cases.

The cedar logs are sawed

into thin, narrow strips called **slats**.

These are also about 7¼ inches long,

the same as the leads.

Rounded grooves are cut into the slats,

and glue is spread over the grooved sides.

The leads are placed in the grooves.

Then the slats are pressed tightly together with a clamp,

making a kind of sandwich.

When the glue has dried, the clamp is taken off
and the slat and lead sandwich is cut
into the shapes of pencils.
Then the pencils are sanded smooth and painted.
Finally, erasers are put on.

Colored pencils are made in much the same way as lead pencils, but colorful dyes are used instead of graphite. However, only lead pencils can be erased cleanly.

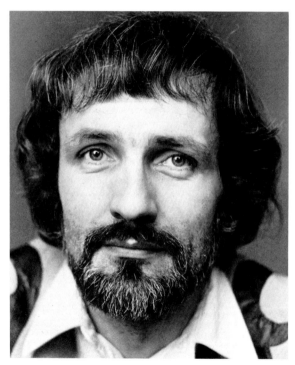

Ali
Mitgutsch

ALI MITGUTSCH is one of Germany's best-known
children's book illustrators. He is a devoted world traveler, and
many of his book ideas have taken shape during his travels.
Perhaps this is why they have such international appeal.
Mr. Mitgutsch's books have been published in 22 countries
and are enjoyed by thousands of readers around the world.

Ali Mitgutsch lives with his wife and three children in
Schwabing, the artists' quarter in Munich. The Mitgutsch
family also enjoys spending time on their farm in the Bavarian
countryside.

THE CAROLRHODA
⋙ START

TO FINISH ⋙
BOOKS